St Teilo

C000178250

National Museum Wales Books

First published in 2007 by National Museum Wales Books, Cathays Park, Cardiff, CF10 3NP, Wales. Reprinted in 2008, 2011.

ISBN 978-0-7200-0589-9

Text: Sara Huws, Gerallt Nash
Design: Peter Gill & Associates

This book is published to mark the official opening of St Teilo's Church at St Fagans: National History Museum, as part of Amgueddfa Cymru – National Museum Wales's centenary celebrations in 2007.

We wish to acknowledge the invaluable assistance offered by external specialists including Dr Madeleine Gray, the Rev. Anthony Parkinson, Dr John Morgan-Guy, Daveth Frost, Alun Adams, the Rev. John Walters and Mrs Madge O'Keefe, as well as colleagues at Amgueddfa Cymru. We also wish to acknowledge the help and support of members of the community at Pontarddulais, the 1520 Group (Wales and the Marches Catholic History Society), staff at the Royal Commission on the Ancient and Historical Monuments of Wales and the Archaeology Department at Cardiff University.

Sponsored by
Welsh Assembly
Government

Contents

Foreword

In 1508 a young sculptor was asked to stop the job he was doing and paint a ceiling instead. He spent the next four years painting what is recognized as one of the world's greatest masterpieces. The artist was called Michelangelo Buonarroti, his client was the Pope, and the ceiling he painted was that of the Sistine Chapel in Rome.

Some ten years later another craftsman was decorating the walls of another church, that of Llandeilo Tal-y-bont in south Wales. We do not know his name, and never will. But we can now see in all its glory what he and his fellows did in this typical Welsh parish church for, uniquely, it has been re-erected and redecorated as it would have looked in the 1520s.

St Fagans is famous for its re-erected buildings. In this instance, we decided that displaying the process was as important as completing the re-erection, which explains why it has taken a good few years to reach this point. All the surviving original materials have been re-used and missing items have been researched by experts, so that everything is as it would have been. Floor tiles and glass, altar furnishings and furniture have all been meticulously recreated. A new, hand-carved rood screen was made and decorated, and the walls covered in paintings – perhaps the greatest shock to us today.

The result is a triumph of traditional craft skills, and a tribute to the craftsmen of the past and present alike. In its own way it is as striking as the Sistine Chapel.

Dr Eurwyn Wiliam
Deputy Director General,
Amgueddfa Cymru –
National Museum Wales

Where did St Teilo's Church come from?

St Teilo's Church was originally built on the banks of the river Llwchwr, near Pontarddulais. 'The old church on the marsh', as it was fondly called on its original site, is dedicated to St Teilo. He was a popular saint and a contemporary of St David, the Welsh patron saint, and parishes bearing his name are to be found across south Wales. The full name of the parish is Llandeilo Tal-y-bont, which roughly translates as 'the parish (or church) dedicated to St Teilo, by the crossing-point of the river'. Though there is no longer a bridge near the site, it has been suggested that the Church might have been on one of the main routes through south Wales, possibly for pilgrims on their way to St Davids. It is easy to imagine travellers entering the Church to pray for safe passage across the tidal waters of the River Llwchwr. Paintings of St Christopher, who is associated with safe travel and pilgrimage, were discovered in the Church. The Church played a central role in medieval life, and was one of the only large meeting places available to the community. Even the churchyard was a setting for festivals, fairs and sports. The influence of religion was exceptionally strong on all aspects of day-to-day life in the Middle Ages. People believed that everything from sickness, poverty, health or prosperity, to the failure or success of crops, was the result of whether or not they were good Christians. The Church's rich and intricate decoration was representative of the glory that awaited the good Christian in heaven, and would also have served as a diversion from the Latin mass performed there every Sunday. Because of its central and complex place in daily life, the Church was filled with countless symbols, images and messages, all intricately woven into the decorative scheme.

There was probably a church at this location before the Normans arrived in Wales, and the dedication to St Teilo suggests that there was a *clas* or religious community established here, possibly as early as the seventh century. The earliest parts of the present church, the nave and chancel, might date back to the twelfth or early thirteenth century, as does the font.

During the fourteenth or early fifteenth century, two chapels were built onto the Church, creating a cruciform or cross-shaped plan.

Previous page: Recreating the medieval wall-paintings.
Left: A photograph of the Church in its original location, showing the south aisle and porch.

During the mid to late fifteenth century, the building was extended along the south side to form an aisle. This meant demolishing the original south wall of the nave and replacing it with two arches. A timber rood screen and loft were also built. Between the years 1500 and 1540, the interior was repainted, this time with scenes from the Passion Cycle, together with images of popular saints such as St Christopher, St Thomas Becket, St James and St Margaret. Finally, a porch was added, leading to the south aisle.

Some time during or after the Reformation, the rood screen and loft were removed, and the wall-paintings were painted over. Major works were carried out in 1810, which included the installation of box pews and a three-decker covered pulpit in the nave as part of a re-arrangement of the interior. Most of the old windows had been removed by this time and had been replaced by large, lancet-shaped windows. The building ceased functioning as the parish church in 1852, when a new parish church, also named St Teilo's, was built in nearby Pontarddulais. The old church remained in use for burials and occasional services, but even these came to an end in 1973. The building then fell into rapid decay. The slate roof tiles were stolen, leaving the structure exposed and compromised. Efforts to conserve the building in situ by finding a new use for it proved unsuccessful, and in 1982 the Church in Wales offered the building, which had served the parish of Llandeilo Tal-y-bont for some 800 years, to the Museum for re-erection at St Fagans.

Previous pages:
(Left, above) The Church's exterior, photographed in 1984;
(left, below) The east wall of the aisle, with traces of the medieval wall-paintings just visible;
(right) The south aisle, photographed in 1984.
Right and overleaf: Part of the hand-carved double vine-trail incorporating the story of Teilo's life.

10

Who was Teilo?

Teilo was born about AD 500, in Penally, Pembrokeshire. He studied in Whitland under the learned scholar Paulinus, and embarked on a life of religious devotion.

His ministry took him not only around large parts of Wales, but also to Cornwall and Brittany. Though many parishes still bear his name, there are very few legends associated with him in Wales. However, many wonderful tales and representations of Teilo survive in Brittany. For example, the *troménie* of St Teilo, an ancient procession of his relics around a parish, is still performed in the village of Landeleau to this day.

The story of Teilo's life can be seen on the Church's rood loft. It depicts the most popular legends about the saint in twenty-five scenes, all hand-carved from a single solid piece of oak.

Why is the Church now in St Fagans?

St Fagans: National History Museum has been at the forefront of rescuing, recording, moving and re-erecting buildings since it opened to the public in 1948. Threatened buildings are given a new lease of life in a sensitive and relevant context, and our understanding of life in the past is greatly enhanced by the process. In the case of St Teilo's Church, our masons, carpenters and painters used the same tools, materials and techniques as were employed hundreds of years ago, hence building on an already extensive reservoir of skills. Attempts to restore the building in situ had been hampered by subsidence, periodic flooding and its remote location. The decision was made, therefore, to move the building before it was too late.

Left and above: Rebuilding the roof.
Above right: Traditional tools were
used to carve new stone window
tracery, to replace the missing
sections.

15

Left: The painstaking work
of uncovering the medieval
wall-paintings.

Moving, rebuilding and refurbishing a stone-built medieval church presented quite a challenge for the Museum's specialist Historic Buildings Unit, and this is possibly the first time that such a project has been attempted in Europe. The attention to detail has been meticulous, and all restoration has been informed by current academic and scientific research. Where parts were broken or missing, they have been repaired or re-created by skilled museum craftsmen, using the same sorts of tools, materials and techniques that were used in the Middle Ages. This painstaking process of dismantling and rebuilding has spanned more than 20 years; the result is a triumph of craftsmanship, colour and imagery. The opening of the Church in 2007 in its new home at St Fagans represents another chapter in a history that extends back almost 1,400 years to the time of St Teilo himself.

Left: Applying gold leaf by hand to the rood screen.

Moving a medieval church

Before dismantling began, the building was carefully measured and recorded. Hundreds of photographs were taken at every stage of the process. When we were satisfied that all the wall-paintings had been removed, any remaining plaster, limewash and render was picked off by hand to reveal the stonework beneath. Every window and door, and all structural features, were allocated an identification letter.

Each associated stone was then numbered, measured and recorded individually. The roof timbers were also measured, and their positions noted.

Once all the elements of the building had been checked and recorded, the work of dismantling the building began. More than 200 tonnes of stone and timber were transported to the Museum.

Why 1520?

Our reconstruction shows how the Church may have appeared about 1520. We chose this date for several reasons, not least because the Church had grown to its present size and layout by that time, but also because the majority of the wall-paintings uncovered at the site had been painted by then.

It was also a particularly important period in Welsh history, leading up to the Reformation and the replacement of Roman Catholicism as the official religion of the country, and the Acts of Union, which would unite Wales and England under the rule of Henry VIII.

The walls

The numbered stone walls were carefully rebuilt using lime mortar. The stone foundations extended for more than a metre below the ground. Using traditional timber supports, or formwork, the five large arches in the nave and chancel were re-erected. The bell-cote was also restored to its original medieval appearance.

Left above and below: Rebuilding the arches, using traditional techniques.
Above: The coursed stonework in the churchyard wall.

The windows

Most of the medieval carved stone windows were probably removed during a remodelling of the Church in 1810. Fortunately, a few pieces of original window tracery were uncovered when the Church was being dismantled. These were used as patterns by the masons who carved the new stonework for the windows.

The glass for the windows was researched and installed by members of the Welsh School of Architectural Glass in Swansea. The panes are made of hand-blown green glass, typical of the Tudor period. The north-west window of the church is believed to be earlier than many of the others, and so has been glazed in an earlier type of cloudy blue glass associated with the fourteenth and fifteenth centuries.

Left: Stone repairs to an early fourteenth-century window.
Right: Where original stonework had been removed, replica period details have been incorporated.

The roof

All the main roof timbers were made of oak and, wherever possible, we have re-used the original trusses. Each timber truss was first examined and tested to make sure that it was still capable of supporting a stone-tiled roof. Sadly, some were so badly affected by rot or insect attack that they had to be discarded. Other, less decayed timbers were saved by inserting pieces of new oak to replace the affected parts. New trusses were made for the nave and chancel. However, all but one of the trusses in the north chapel are original, as are more than half the trusses in the south aisle. The best place to see the repair work close-up is in the porch, where old and new sit together.

For the new parts of the roof, oak was bought from sources in north and east Wales. Each timber was cut to shape using traditional hand tools – chisels, mallets and saws. Mortise and tenon joints were cut to create strong 'A' frames, and fixed into place by thick wooden pegs. The timbers were then trimmed smooth using an adze, giving the wood its distinctive hand-finished look. Finally, a decorative moulding was carved on the underside of each truss. The structure as it stands supports the weight of about forty-five tonnes of sandstone tiles. Each of these tiles was individually pegged in place, as can be seen in the porch.

Left: The oak roof trusses ready to be lifted into position on the nave.

The bell

The new bell was cast in 2006 by Taylor, Eayre & Smith, Bell Founders of Loughborough. They are best known for casting the largest bell in Britain – Great Paul in St Paul's Cathedral, in 1881. Though of more modest proportions, our bell has also been cast using centuries-old techniques, and a design based on a fifteenth-century bell found in St Illtyd's Church in Llantwit Major. Like many medieval bells, it has a prayer in Latin around the crown: "SANCTE TELIAUE ORA PRO NOBIS", which translates as 'St Teilo, pray for us'.

Above and right: The bell was specially cast to a medieval pattern.

The rood screen and carvings

Before the Reformation, nearly all churches had a screen of some description, which served primarily to separate ordinary people from the holiest part of the church, the chancel.

The screen now seen in St Teilo's Church was designed and carved by the Museum's Head Carpenter, Ray Smith. It is based on surviving examples from Glamorgan, with a central doorway flanked by two openings on either side. Above is the rood loft, the front of which is decorated with two rows of elaborately carved vine-trails. One of these trails incorporates the life of St Teilo. The twelve carved panels feature paintings of the Apostles. They incorporate designs and colours that were popular at the time, as well as motifs such as the Tudor rose.

Along the top of the loft is a 'rood beam', on which sculptures of Christ on the Cross (the Crucifix, or 'Rood'), the Virgin Mary and John the Evangelist are mounted. These would have served as a focal point for worshippers. Very few of these carved crucifixes survived the destruction of the Reformation, and we are lucky to have two in our collections – one of which can be seen in the Oriel 1 gallery at St Fagans.

Left and overleaf: Carving the panels for the rood loft.
Above: Preliminary colour trials, incorporating gold leaf.

37

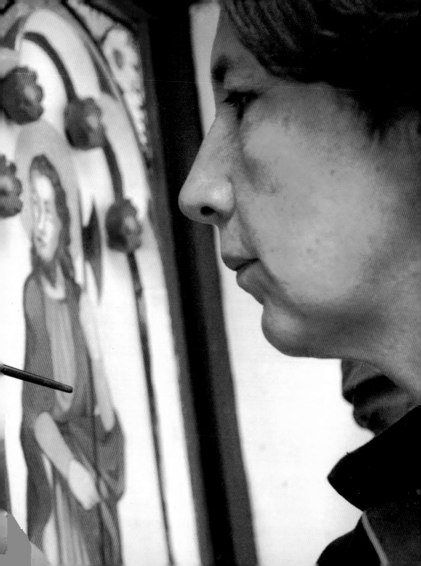

On the right-hand side of the main (or high) altar is a statue of the Madonna (or Virgin) and Child, and on the left is a statue of St Teilo. Very few original carvings of this type survive in Britain.

We therefore looked to Brittany, where medieval carvings of the Madonna and Teilo can still be found. These were then used by specialist master carver Emyr Hughes as patterns when carving our statues.

In medieval times, the carved woodwork would have been painted with bright colours and patterns. Red, green, white, yellow and blue were popular colours, with fine details often picked out in gold leaf. Diagonal 'barber pole' and geometric chequerboard patterns were popular. Features such as the carved vine trails were gilded, with the leaves, grapes and other details being coloured or glazed. The strong nautical links between north Devon and south Wales in the period led to a shared tradition; this meant that we could base some of our painted images on examples found in that area.

Previous page: Recreating the paintings for the rood loft.
Above: A detail of the painted panels on the rood loft, showing the Apostles.
Right: Carving the story of Teilo, for inclusion above the rood screen.

The Reformation

Originating in sixteenth-century Germany, the Reformation was a series of protests aimed at changing the structure of worship, and of the Catholic Church. Those opposed to the status quo believed that the Pope's regime was greedy and sinful, and sought to purify the Christian movement according to the Ten Commandments. Though it was a gradual change, which affected the whole of northern Europe in some form, the destruction and eradication of images and carvings was particularly thorough in those countries that adopted Protestantism as the main religion. Statues of Christ and the Virgin Mary were destroyed, as were paintings such as those found hidden in Llandeilo Tal-y-bont.

The wall-paintings

When the building was moved to St Fagans, it was only natural that the paintings came too. They had remained hidden for centuries under layers of limewash, which had to be removed using doctors' scalpels. Each image, including the plaster on which it had been painted, had to be physically removed from the walls, a process that took three months. Experts from the Archaeology Department at Cardiff University were able to stabilise and conserve the wall-paintings. Close analysis revealed the techniques and colours used by the medieval artists almost 500 years ago. The original wall-paintings were too fragile to be put back, so we painted exact copies onto the walls. Missing areas were recreated using evidence drawn from contemporary illustrations, stained glass and other surviving paintings in Wales and elsewhere. Before the Reformation, all churches would have been painted with Biblical scenes, saints, angels, texts and patterns.

The original painting scheme at St Teilo's would have been vibrant and rich, showing scenes of pain and sacrifice, as well as of the glory of heaven and the majesty of the Christian Trinity.

The paints used in the recreation are based on traditional paint recipes. Most of the coloured powders or pigments used are derived from ochres, oxides, plant dyes and mineral compounds. These are then mixed with different natural binders to give the paint different qualities, such as the thick, shiny glaze on the rood loft, and the matt, earth tones of the wall-paintings.

The paintings close-up

One surviving painting pre-dates all the others. St Catherine (right) was painted around 1400, and is currently on display in Oriel 1. She is shown, dressed in late fourteenth-century costume, standing next to a spiked wheel (on which she was tortured – giving name to the 'Catherine wheel') and holding a sword, by which she was executed for her Christian beliefs. She is the patron saint of scholars, nurses, potters, wheelwrights and engineers. One of the most complete scenes was 'The Mocking of Christ' (page 47), now seen reproduced above one of the windows in the nave. Two accusers stand on either side of Christ, and large droplets of spit, or venom, can be seen flying from their mouths and onto his face. Many church paintings from this period show different aspects of the Passion – the story of Jesus Christ's Crucifixion and Resurrection.

This scene shows a serene Christ, enduring mental as well as physical torture, before he is nailed to the cross.

An unexpected find

During the work, the youngest
member of the Historic Buildings
Unit found a stone carved with a
cross among the wall masonry.
It is believed to date back to
sometime between the seventh
and ninth centuries. It was further
embellished, possibly in the
eleventh century, into a shield-
like design. This stone therefore
pre-dates the earliest parts of the
present church.

Visiting St Teilo's Church

Visitors are asked not to touch the wall-paintings, carved screens or any items displayed in the Church, and to treat the building with respect.

Please be aware that we sometimes have to close displays for conservation reasons.

A range of pre-booked activities are provided. Contact the Education Office on (029) 2057 3403 for further information on group activities.

You can check *What's On*, our events listings, and our website (www.museumwales.ac.uk) to find out about special events and talks relating to St Teilo's Church.

Thank you

We are grateful to the following funders for their generous contributions towards the cost of the re-erection of the Church and for many of the items within it.

The G. C. Gibson Charitable Trust
The Jane Hodge Foundation
S. R. & P. H. Southall Charitable Trust

THE
HEADLEY
TRUST

Anne Morris and Janet Davies
Desmond Perkins
Audrey Perkins

The following Patrons of
Amgueddfa Cymru –
National Museum Wales:

Dr Margaret Berwyn Jones
David and Carole Burnett
Mary Cashmore
Margaret Davies
Gerard and Elisabeth Elias
Sir Patrick and Lady Elias
Dr Margaret Elmes

Sigi and Wynford Evans CBE
Roger and Kathy Farrance CBE
Bob and Chris Forster
Pearl Gayther
E. M. W. Griffith
Sir Richard Hanbury-Tenison KCVO
Alan and Judith Hart
G. Wyn Howells, Miss Marion
Evans and Mrs Wynne Evans
Jane Jenkins
Ian and Julia Kelsall
K. Pat Kernick
Lord Kinnock
Capt. Norman Lloyd Edwards
Pat Long
L. Hefin Looker
Paul and Lynne Loveluck
Malcolm and Monica Porter
The Rt Hon. the Lord Rees QC
Dr Paul M. Smith
Ken and Fran Truman
David and Chris Vokes
Dr Peter Warren CBE
Dr Jane Watkeys
John and Hilary Weber
Richard Weston and Linda Prosper
Dr David and Dr Val Williams
Gareth and Ruth Williams
Derek and Joan Woolley